Contents

Introduction

Britain today is a country made up of many different groups of people, from a wide variety of backgrounds and cultures, with different beliefs and attitudes. Differences between people can challenge us and allow us to experience new cultures and ideas. For some people this can be threatening, for others it is something worth celebrating. How did it come to be this way? How can we learn to live together in the future? In this book we will look at some of the many cultures that make up Britain today, and begin to explore some of the challenges that face us now and in the years ahead.

Who are we?

Have you got a passport? I have just been looking at mine. On the front are the words: **European Community** and **United Kingdom of Great Britain and Northern Ireland**. Inside the back cover there is my name, a statement that I am a British citizen, my date of birth, and the town where I was born. On the same page of the passport there is a photograph of me to help customs officers and others to connect this passport with the person carrying it.

All these things are part of my **identity**. They are all part of how I see myself and how other people see me. There are, of course, many more things that make up my identity – some are things that only I, or people close to me, know about. So my identity is partly public and partly private. But added all together it makes – me!

In my case, my passport tells everyone that I am British, and that I was born in Britain. But what does it mean to be British? Some people would say that being British means sharing a common language (English), a common history, a

Typically 'British'? A still from the once-popular TV series, *The Avengers*: Diana Rigg and Patrick Macnee with vintage car.